Anna and Rosa's Bicycle Stories

Design by Christopher Jowett

Book first published 2023

Published by Crilatus Books

Printed by Book Empire
www.bookempire.co.uk
Unit 7, Lotherton Way, Garforth, Leeds, LS25 2JY

Printed in Great Britain

ISBN 978-1-7395031-0-9

Foreword

Anna and Rosa are two young bicycles who live in the valley of Cristo. They live in a shed next to the Post Office and belong to Pat and Penny, the two daughters of Mr and Mrs Stamp, the Postmaster and his wife. Cars and lorries are not allowed in the valley so bicycles are used by everyone. Bicycles in Cristo are rather special, for not only can they speak to each other but, also, to the children. Although adults knew this when they were young, they don't believe it now they are grown up.

The only way into the valley is by railway or walking by the fast-flowing stream. The summer is warm and spectacular waterfalls tumble over the rocky cliffs, the winter is cold and snowy, ideal for skiing.

Anna is a medium size bicycle and is always careful. Rosa is smaller and is curious to know what is going on. Many of the stories are set in Cristo but some adventures mean travelling to the main line train station and the airport.

Each story is written using the readers own imagination as most people will relate to the characters. The pictures included are to support the stories and give the reader backgrounds in which to set their imagination. These are the images I used when writing the stories, plus a few I made up.

Contents

The Author

It's always the same. Christmas and New Year are in the past and the days are slowly getting longer. Time to think about a summer holiday. Without knowing where I wanted to go, a trip to the Travel Agent seemed like a good idea, all those brochures will give me some ideas.

The local Travel Agent had been in business for many years and the door still had a little bell which tinkled when you opened it.

"Good morning," said the Travel Agent.

"Hello," I replied. "I am looking for somewhere to go on holiday."

"Well you have come to the right place! What type of holiday would you like and where would you like to go?" asked the Travel Agent.

"I don't fancy a big hotel with a swimming pool and night club, a cruise is possible but usually expensive," I said.

"How about mountains and lakes?" said the Travel Agent.

"That sounds interesting. What is there?" I asked.

"The brochures are on the bottom shelf, over there, help yourself," said the Travel Agent.

"Thank you," I said picking up three glossy brochures.

Later at home, came the job of reading what each hotel had to offer, where it was and what the weather might be like.

"This looks interesting," I thought. "Cristo is a mountain village surrounded by beautiful snow-capped mountains. Accessible only by train or mountain footpath, this quiet village has plenty to offer all travellers. I'll ask the Travel Agent to book it for me."

A few weeks later an envelope arrived from the Travel Agent confirming my booking for one week in Cristo.

The months passed slowly, until the day finally arrived to travel. First to the airport, a flight, a large express train and finally a small local train.

With a little toot on the whistle, the train slowly moved out of the big station, along a narrow track and out into the countryside, with fields of grass, tall trees and huge mountains all around. As the valley got narrower the fast flowing stream crashed over the rocks and the sunlight was broken by the tall trees. I wondered what would be at the end of this enchanting journey.

I gasped with surprise as the train turned the last corner of the twisting track, the trees cleared and the village of Cristo came into sight. The train stopped and I thought. "This is beautiful." I pulled my little suitcase along the platform, past the ticket office to the waiting visitor train.

"Anymore for Cristo?" shouted a man standing next to the carriages. "Please take your seats, you can walk if you want but I wouldn't recommend it with a suitcase." He said looking at me.

I lifted up my suitcase, sat on the bench and with a jolt backwards, then forwards, we slowly moved up the hill. On to the main street and with another jolt we stopped.

"Well, what a day, a taxi, a plane, two trains and this. I wonder what the rest of the week will bring?" I murmured to myself, as the little wheels of the suitcase rumbled along the road to the Peak View Hotel.

The door was open and behind a small desk sat a lady wearing glasses attached to a long chain that stops you from losing them.

"Hello, I have a booking at your hotel," I said.

"Oh yes we were expecting you. My name is Mrs Guest and I am the owner of the Peak View Hotel, welcome," she said.

"I am booked for one week, bed, breakfast and evening meal," I said.

"Yes, that's right, I have given you the best room with beautiful views of the mountains," said Mrs Guest.

I went upstairs, unpacked and sat on the balcony until it was time for dinner. There were just a few people staying at this small hotel, and after a lovely meal and feeling very tired from travelling I decided to go straight to bed.

It always takes a while to get to sleep in a strange bed, even though I was tired. I wonder what tomorrow would bring, but it wasn't long before I was fast asleep.

"What to do first. Explore the village and then perhaps a walk up the valley," I thought. "What I need is a map then I won't get lost, I'll try the Post Office."

The Post Office was full of everything you might ever need, especially souvenirs, but where are the maps?"

"Excuse me," I said to the Postmaster. "Do you have any maps?"

"Yes, they are over there next to the birthday cards," said the Postmaster.

Having picked up a map and paid, I set off along the Main Street. With the map open and looking like a tourist I went in search of buildings marked on the map.

"There's the Cycle Hire Shop, the Post Office I've just been to, so down there should be the school and the road along the valley," I mumbled to myself.

I had been walking for about ten minutes when I heard the sound of heavy breathing, I turned to see a very large man riding a bicycle.

"Poor bicycle," I said in a quiet voice as they passed.

"Easy for you to say," came the reply.

"I wasn't expecting a reply and was puzzled. Oh well, keep walking," I thought.

A bit further along the road I heard two girls talking. Nothing in particular just girl talk. When I turned the corner, there sat on a wooden bench, was a girl and a bicycle.

"Hello," I said. "I thought I heard you talking to someone?"

"Oh hello, you must be the man staying with Mrs Guest, my name is Pat, I live at the Post Office and this is my bicycle Anna," said Pat.

"Yes, that's right I'm on holiday. Do you talk to your bicycle?" I asked.

"Yes," said Anna. "All the children can talk to their bicycles.

"But grown-ups can't hear," said Pat. "Except Father Christmas and now you. How can that be?"

"I don't know," I said. "Oh well I'd best be on my way. Bye Pat and Anna."

After walking a bit further I stopped for a rest under a large oak tree.

I was suddenly woken by the sound of an alarm clock. Well that was an interesting dream. Fancy children that can talk to bicycles. I got up and spent 10 minutes admiring the view from my bedroom balcony.

After a breakfast of warm bread with homemade jam together with fresh coffee, I went outside to look round the village.

"I'd better buy a map, so I don't get lost," I thought. "The Post Office might have some. The Post Office was full of souvenirs and lots of things you never thought you would need.

"Where are the maps?" I wondered.

"Next to the birthday cards," came a voice from behind the counter.

"How did you know I wanted a map?" I said.

"Oh, the first thing visitors want is a map," said the Postmaster.

I paid and went outside just in time to see a very large man collect a bicycle from Mr Wheeler's Cycle Hire Shop. I stopped, frozen to the spot.

"My dream is repeating, I must do something different," I thought. "I know I will hire a bicycle."

I looked at the list of bicycles and the prices in the window of the shop and went in.

"Hello, I would like to hire a bicycle for a week," I said.

"Very good," said Mr Wheeler. "What type of bicycle would you like? I would recommend something strong, perhaps a mountain bike."

"That sounds good, I'll have a mountain bike," I said. "How about that one?"

Mr Wheeler began writing my details in his book, where I was staying and the bicycle I was hiring.

"There that's, that done, please sign here," he said. "The date of return is on your copy, or leave it with Mrs Guest and I will collect next week."

It may seem obvious now, but at the time I never gave a thought, to the fact I hadn't ridden a bicycle for a long time. They say you never forget how to ride a bicycle, but believe me practice is required after a long break.

"Well mountain bike, you are stuck with me all week so let's take it easy to start with," I said quietly.

This way. There's the Post Office, next should be the school, then the road along the valley. I had a sense that I had done this before and again after a few minutes I heard a voice of a girl talking to herself, I turned the corner and there, on the bench, was a girl and a bicycle.

"Hello," I said. "I thought I heard you talking to someone?"

"Oh hello! You must be the man staying with Mrs Guest. My name is Pat, I live at the Post Office and this is my bicycle Anna," said Pat.

"Have we met before?" I asked.

"No," replied Pat.

"Well, I dreamt last night that you were sitting here talking to your bicycle. In the dream I could hear what you were both saying," I said.

Pat looked at Anna, then, they both looked at me.

"What do you do?" asked Pat. "And why have you come to Cristo?"

"I write stories for children and my hobby is photography. I have always liked mountain holidays and Cristo looked very nice place in the brochure," I replied. "Why do you ask?"

"Can you keep a secret?" asked Pat.

"Yes of course," I said.

"Well, your dream is coming true," said Pat. "The children and bicycles in Cristo can talk to each other but, as we get older and become grown up we can't except..!"

"Father Christmas," I said.

"Yes, that's right and now maybe you," said Pat. "There is a legend that one day a writer will come to Cristo and discover the secret, writing many stories for children."

"But I can only hear you, not Anna," I said.

"Can you hear Bill?" asked Pat.

"Who's Bill?" I asked.

"You are sitting on Bill, the mountain bike," said Pat.

I looked down at the mountain bike and saw the name Bill written on the frame.

"Oh Bill, no I haven't heard him say anything," I said.

"Probably a good job, he thinks you are overweight," said Pat.

"Really," I said. "Mr Wheeler did recommend something strong. Well Bill, I guess I will be riding you a lot more, to get plenty of exercise."

"Oh no, now look what you've done," said Bill.

Pat and Anna began laughing.

"Wait, stop a moment," I said. "I heard that. Say something else, Bill?"

"Fatso," said Bill.

"How rude," I said. "I really can hear. You need to be more careful of what you say."

"You are the writer who has come to make us famous, we must go and tell Penny and Rosa!" said Anna.

"But I need to know more," I said.

"Oh you will, let's meet here again tomorrow about the same time," said Pat as she pedalled toward the village.

"Right Bill, let's get some exercise," I said.

"Yes, let's see if you really can remember how to ride a bicycle," said Bill.

The rest of the morning was spent cycling along the flat part of the valley, stopping from time to time to take photographs. After buying a sandwich and a drink from the ski lift shop, Bill and I finally stopped to rest under a large tree. Being a writer you never know when a story will come to mind, a small idea, or a small picture that might tell a story. For that reason I always carry a note book and camera, just in case.

I made a few notes about what Pat had said and asked Bill. "You're a hire bicycle, you must have plenty of stories to tell."

"It's a busy life being a hire bicycle," said Bill. "Most of the time people are like you, they just want a gentle cycle ride along the valley. You know to get some exercise."

"Okay, can we stop the overweight jokes. You must have had heavier people than me," I said.

Bill chattered on and on about his life and stories of the other hicycles as hire bicycles refer to themselves, so much so that I filled my note book.

"Bill," I said. "We should be getting back to Cristo. I have filled my only note book and need to get another. The Post Office should sell some."

With everything packed up and my sandwich wrapper in the bin we set off. As I pedalled Bill worked the gears and surprisingly we arrived at the Post Office very quickly. The Post Office only sold children's school note books so I bought three of those and with Bill safely inside the shed at the Peak View Hotel, I went for dinner then went to bed.

The following day I met Pat's sister, Penny and her bicycle Rosa.

"Hello, nice to meet you," I said. "Has Pat told you about me?"

"Yes, it all sounds very exciting!" said Penny. "We are thinking about giving you a special Cristo experience."

"Oh yes," I said with a hesitant tone in my voice. "Does this involve riding a bicycle by any chance?"

"Yes, how did you guess?" said Pat. "But you have to be fit."

"Some more exercises I guess, okay. What do I have to do?" I asked.

"Well we have entered you for the Cristo Mountain Bike Challenge," said Penny. "It was my idea, you know, just to get you started on your first story."

"When is this challenge?" I asked.

"On Saturday," replied Bill. "But don't worry I have done the course many times and you have three days to practice."

At that point I realised there was no way out of the challenge, and the more practice I had, the better.

"Okay show me what I have to do," I said.

Pat and Penny and the three bicycles became very excited about having someone to train, and before I had chance to rethink we were all pedalling along the valley road. Bill expertly showed me the way round the course, along woodland tracks, through streams and worst of all, the steep hills. After a very exhausting run Penny gave us our times.

"If this had been the time last year, everyone would be at home eating their dinner," said Pat. "Tomorrow you must try harder."

Saturday soon arrived and after a light breakfast I collected Bill and met Pat and Penny.

"I've given you a number near the end so you won't feel you are being chased by expert riders," said Penny.

"Thank you," I said. "I'm number 23, at 2 minute intervals that means three quarters of an hour."

"Yes, so you keep calm and stop playing with the gears," said Bill. "I will do that."

I watched as other riders wearing tight fitting clothes get ready. Lots of stretching exercises and a cycling machine to get warmed up on, this was serious stuff.

I was lost in my thoughts and wondering if this was another dream when coach, Pat said, "Okay, you're on soon. Time to get warmed up. Let's do a few stretches, that's right, now touch your toes."

I looked at Pat and said, "Touch my toes, no chance! Bending will have to do."

"Star jumps. Right that will have to do, you're next," said Pat.

With that I pushed Bill to the starting line and showing no signs of fear, I sat on the saddle. Not having any skin tight clothing I had to make do with some old football shorts, trainers and T shirt Penny gave me.

"Right Bill, it's you and me," I said.

"Yup, we're not going to win but let's not be last," said Bill.

"Five, four, three, two, one, go," said the starter, off we went.

I knew the course well, having practised during the week but, somehow it did feel easier and soon we came off the road and onto the woodland trail.

Bill shouted out instructions, "Up gear, down gear, left, left, now right, mind the tree." This was clearly a bicycle that knew what to do.

"Just the stream and the hill to go," I thought. "Then to my surprise we saw number 22 ahead struggling up the hill.

"Look Bill we're catching up," I shouted.

"Yes," shouted Bill. "Now shut up and pedal."

"Bossy bike," I thought, but at least we wouldn't be last.

Once over the hill, it was round the marker, and a straight run down the hill to Cristo, and the finishing line. Bill clicked through the gears and we got faster and faster.

"Put your head down, it will help the speed," shouted Bill.

I did what he said, and with the T-shirt flapping in the wind, and the people cheering, I finished just behind number 20. I don't know what happened to number 21.

"We did it," I shouted exhausted and excited.

Slowly we stopped next to Pat and Penny.

"Well done you two," said Pat. "That was brilliant, I don't know what time was, but it was good."

"I need to lie down for a while," I said.

"Just move around and let your muscles slowly relax." continued Pat.

I did as I was told and watched as the last riders come across the finishing line.

"Now all we have to do is wait," said Bill. "It will be about 3 o'clock when they announce the winners."

Just as Bill had been right about everything else so it was. At 3 o'clock the speaker whistled into life and the voice said, "Ladies and Gentlemen, boys and girls, here are the results of the Cristo Mountain Bike Challenge. There were 28 entrants and 25 finished. In third place with a time 18 minutes and 52 seconds and last year's winner, number 1.

In second place with a time of 18 minutes and 5 seconds is number 6 and this year's winner and a new record with a time of 17 minutes and 45 seconds is number 3."

A big cheer went up and everyone clapped their hands as number 3 went to collect the trophy.

"Congratulations to everyone and if you would like to come forward and collect your certificate and get your time," said the voice.

"Go on," said Penny. "Go get yours."

I left Bill leaning against a tree and walked stiffly across to the table and collected a rather nice certificate and a badge. Feeling very pleased with myself I met Pat and Penny and the bicycles.

"Well, what did you get?" asked Pat.

"Oh not too bad," I said.

"What's not too bad?" asked Penny.

"Well, the time was 23 minutes and 16 seconds and I came twelfth," I said.

"That's pretty good for a fatso," said Bill. "Or should I say, not a fatso."

We all smiled and walked back to the hotel where a long warm soak awaited. My week in Cristo was almost over, not a holiday I had planned but very enjoyable.

By the time I came to leave Cristo most people had heard about the writer and there was a small crowd to say goodbye as I waited for the train. My suitcase was a little heavier with souvenirs from the Post Office. My rucksack had many more note books and the camera was full of pictures. Bill was back at Mr Wheeler's shop waiting for the next person and Pat and Penny stood with Anna and Rosa.

"Goodbye," I said to Pat and Penny. "This has been a wonderful holiday, you have all made me very welcome. I will write to Pat with any news and you will be the first to read any new stories."

At that moment loud 'Toot' came from the train warning that it was about to leave. I quickly boarded the nearest carriage.

"Bye everyone," I shouted. "See you all again."

Everyone waved as the train slowly moved down the track around the first bend. I sat down and thought, "How can I possibly write about children and bicycles that talk to each other? Well at least I have plenty of pictures for the stories and a certificate."

CRISTO MOUNTAIN
BIKE CHALLENGE

2014

this certificate is awarded to:
Christopher Jowett
Position/Time
Finished 12th, 23 minutes 16 seconds

The Oak Tree

Pat and Penny were sitting in the garden of the Post Office early one Sunday morning, Pat was eating a bowl of cereal and fruit. The air was still and a bit chilly as the sun hadn't yet risen over the mountains.

"You see that tree at the bottom of the garden?" asked Pat.

"Yes," said Penny.

"How old do you think it is?" asked Pat.

"Well, let me think. It's been here all the time I have known," said Penny.

"Just have a guess," said Pat.

"Well, Mrs Page told us at school that you can tell how old a tree is by counting the rings," said Penny.

"I know that, but we can't cut down Dad's tree just to answer the question," said Pat.

"Yes. But. I would have thought," said Penny speaking very slowly like grown-ups do when they don't know what they are talking about. "It would be seventy three years old give or take a couple of years."

"Hmm," thought Pat. "I would have said a bit less but you might be right."

"Why the sudden interest in trees?" asked Penny.

"Mrs Page was telling us about the oak tree in the middle of the valley and that it was very old. I wondered how old our tree was," explained Pat.

"I haven't heard about the oak tree, tell me more," said Penny.

"Nobody knows how old it is really, but some experts say it could be seven hundred years old," said Pat.

"Never. How can a tree live that long? Just think what it could tell us," said Penny.

"The story is that the tree knows everything, how Cristo began, all the people who have lived here and everything they have done," said Pat.

"But a tree doesn't have eyes, or ears, and it can't walk, so how does it know?" asked Penny.

"Well, this is the clever bit. They say the wind tells the tree as it blows through the leaves," said Pat.

"So, when we hear the wind outside, it is really listening to us. When we stand under a tree, the wind whistling and blowing it is telling the tree what has been happening," said Penny.

"Exactly. After seven hundred years that's a lot of knowledge, which is why the tree is called the 'Knowledge Tree'," said Pat.

"Oh, I didn't know it had a name," said Penny. "Can we go and see it?"

"Why not," said Pat. "You go and tell Dad where we are going and I'll get my school bag with the whole story."

Soon Pat and Penny were cycling along the road out of Cristo and telling Anna and Rosa about where they were going.

They cycled past the waterfall to where they could see the tree. A small footpath across the field led to the tree, they stopped and looked up at the tree.

"Wow, this is a big tree," said Penny.

"It doesn't look so big from the road but when you get under the branches it's huge," said Pat.

Anna and Rosa were puzzled about all the interest in a tree and Anna said, "Why are we here? What's so special about this tree?"

Pat told Anna and Rosa what Mrs Page had said about the tree and that it holds all the secrets of Cristo.

"If the tree has all the knowledge how does it tell people?" asked Penny.

"Nobody knows," said Pat. "They say the acorns have small bits of knowledge."

"But acorns can't speak," said Anna.

"No, and you can't read them, or eat them," said Rosa.

"Mr Bull does collect the acorns and feed them to his pigs," said Penny.

"Does that mean the pigs know everything?" asked Anna.

"I've never thought to ask," said Pat.

They stood together looking up at the tree and listening to the wind blowing through the leaves.

"Let's try sitting under the tree and see if it can tell us anything," suggested Pat.

Pat and Penny lent Anna and Rosa against the oak tree. Pat sat to one side and Penny sat on the other side.

"We all need to be quiet and listen," said Pat.

A minute later Penny shouted. "Nothing here.'

"Nothing from me," said Anna.

There was nothing from Rosa.

"We need to wait a bit longer," said Pat.

There was silence while they all listened. Pat opened her school bag to look for the story but could only find her homework book.

"Oh well I suppose I could always do my homework whilst I'm waiting. Maths, I hate maths. Probably because I'm rubbish at it, and algebra, yuk," she muttered to herself.

Question 1, Solve $2x - 37 = 25$. Well, a minus becomes a plus on the other side of the equals sign, so $2x = 25 + 37$ and the 2 goes to the other side but to divide. That means $x = 62$ divided by 2 which is 31, the answer is $x = 31$.

"That was easy," said Pat who continued with the other equations and soon finished them all.

"Well, I surprised myself there. All done in ten minutes. That's a record for me and without asking for Dad's help," said Pat. "What's next English?"

Pat read the question to herself. Poetry. Write a short poem about what you can see from where you are sitting.

"Where I am sitting," she thought. "Well, I can see grass, fields, trees, mountains, sky…"

After thinking for a while Pat wrote:

From where I sit the grass is green,
The mighty oak knows all that has been
There is a path beside the field
By which the bicycles were wheeled
In this valley as far as I can see
Stands only one imposing oak tree
Above the mountains the sky is blue
And the cows all around are doing a poo.

"Hmm. Not sure about the last line," thought Pat. "Maybe:

I wish the tree could tell me all it knew.

All the time Pat had been doing her homework Penny had been sleeping. Anna and Rosa were the only two listening to the tree. When Penny did wake she could hear a voice. "The tree is talking," she thought. "And Father Christmas came, what happened next?" the voice asked.

"I know that voice. It's Rosa, but who is she talking to?" muttered Penny.

Slowly she stood up, rubbed her eyes and walked round the tree to where Rosa was leaning. Penny stopped suddenly, and her mouth was wide open, tried to speak but nothing came out. Rosa was not leaning against the tree but standing up facing the tree.

"That's impossible," thought Penny.

Not only was she standing by herself but also talking to the tree, or at least that's what it looked like. Penny moved further round the tree and said, "Hello." Immediately Rosa fell over.

"Oh, now look what you've done," said Rosa. "They were just telling me all about Father Christmas coming to Cristo and you scared them away."

"What's going on?" said Pat as she came rushing round the tree.

"I was talking to the fairies and Penny frightened them," said Rosa still lying on the ground. "Will someone please pick me up?"

"Don't be silly there is no such thing as fairies," said Pat. "What happened?"

"I saw Rosa standing alone. Then as I walked round the tree and she fell over, like she is now," said Penny.

"Please pick me up," said Rosa.

Penny went across to where Rosa was lying. Picked up her bicycle, checked for scratches and lent her back against the tree.

"Okay," said Pat. "Supposing you are right."

"Which I am," said Rosa.

"Just supposing you did see fairies how come Penny didn't see them?" asked Pat.

"That's easy," said Rosa. "People say fairies don't exist but that is only because people can't see them.

They only appear when you blink, they very cleverly appear when your eyes are closed."

"So if Pat and I close our eyes they will appear?" asked Penny. "Yes," said Rosa. "I can see them because I am not a person."

"Okay, let's try something. Pat and I will go to the other side of the tree and you and Anna can stay at this side," said Pat as she moved Anna next to Rosa.

"Can you hear me?" shouted Pat as she and Penny closed their eyes.

"Yes," said Anna.

"Ask the tree what was in Cristo valley before people came?" asked Pat.

There were a few quite moments while the fairies spoke to Anna.

"They say there was nothing here apart from the trees, the river and there was a creature called Crilatus," said Anna.

"Hmm, interesting," said Pat and Penny together.

"Tell me something about Pat?" asked Penny.

After a long wait and a lot of giggling Rosa said. "Well, Pat doesn't like algebra but she can do them when she tries and she needs to practice poetry more."

Penny looked at Pat and said. "Does that mean anything?"

"Yes, I've just done algebra and poetry for homework," said Pat.

"Anything else?" shouted Penny.

"Yes," said Rosa. "Pat has a boyfriend."

"Oh, I didn't know that," said Penny. "Is it true?"

"Of course not," said Pat. "Wherever could it have got that idea from?"

"You are looking very red in the face. You're blushing!" said Penny.

"Last Sunday, walking near the waterfall," said Rosa.

"Ah well, I can see where the mistake has been," said Pat.

"Holding hands," shouted Anna.

"Okay, enough," said Pat quickly. "Let's change the subject. I believe in the tree and fairies, I just wish I could see them."

"You should lay on your back under the tree and look up into the branches, between the leaves and the sky. Just where the sun shines through," said Anna.

"If you are lucky you might just see a fairy fly past," said Rosa.

Pat and Penny did as suggested and waited and waited.

"I can't see anything, maybe I'm looking in the wrong place," said Penny.

"Look there," said Pat excitedly.

"Where?" said Penny.

"Oh you missed it," laughed Pat. "Just kidding."

Then suddenly in the sunlight just above Pat and Penny's heads appeared a tiny fairy, a bit like a butterfly but with a body, arms and legs.

"Keep very still," said Pat quietly. "And look above my head."

Penny slowly moved her head to look at Pat and sure enough there it was, flying this way and that way, very quickly but no mistake the oak tree fairy was there.

"Oh it's gone," said Pat. "But I did definitely see it. Did you?"

"Yes," said Penny. "It was beautiful and so quick."

"Come on let's go back, I can't wait to tell Peter," said Pat.

"Ah, Peter is it," said Penny.

"Opps, slip of the tongue I meant to say Mum and Dad," said Pat.

As they pedalled across the field and back to the road to Cristo, it began to occur to Pat and Penny that if they went round telling everyone that the story of the oak tree was true and they had seen fairies, people might think they'd been dreaming. So the secret of the tree in Cristo valley remains, but when Pat and Penny need help with their homework they know where to go.

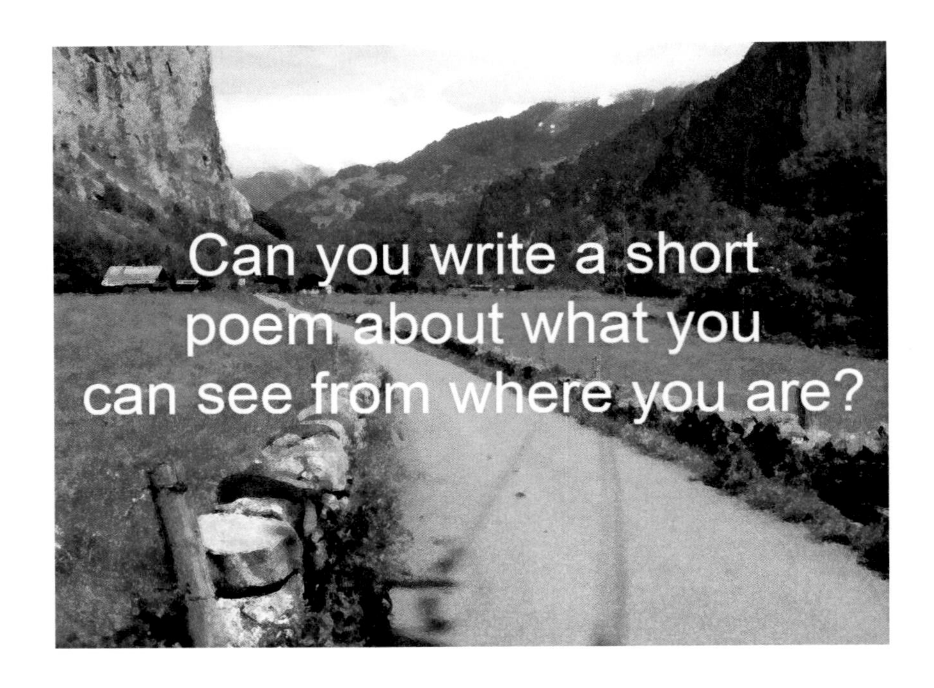

The Treasure Hunt

"Two postcards and stamps, one pen and your change. Thank you," said Mr Stamp to the two ladies in the Post Office who were visiting Cristo for the day.

"At last an empty shop. It's been so busy this afternoon, I think I'll have a sit down for a while," he muttered to himself.

Mr Stamp's rest was suddenly interrupted by shouts of "Dad, Dad," as Pat and Penny came rushing in.

"Dad, can we? Please?" asked Penny.

"Please, Dad, it will be great fun," said Pat excitedly.

"Wait a minute. What are you two getting so excited about?" asked Mr Stamp.

"Here's a letter from school, it tells you all about it. Please say we can go," they said together.

Dear Parent

The school is organising a treasure hunt on Sunday afternoon at 3pm. If your child would like to take part, please sign and return this letter tomorow.

Yours faithfully

Mrs Page
Headteacher

Mr Stamp took the rather crumpled piece of paper that had been stuffed in Pat's pocket and began to read.

"Well, there's no point asking if you would like to go, and it's alright with me, but you must check with your Mum first."

"Brill, thanks Dad," said Pat.

"Brill! Where do they learn these words?" thought Mr Stamp.

Pat and Penny ran out of the Post Office nearly knocking over the new display of souvenir mugs, and almost crashing into a group of day trippers.

After checking with Mrs Stamp, they hurried to tell Anna and Rosa.

Penny pushed open the door of the shed so hard, it crashed into the wall with a loud BANG!

"Oh," shrieked Anna and Rosa as they jumped with fright.

"Guess what you two?" shouted Penny excitedly.

"We're going on a treasure hunt, isn't it brill!" exclaimed Pat.

"And you can come too," added Penny.

"What's a treasure hunt?" asked Anna.

"Well, what happens is this," explained Pat. "The teachers hide pieces of paper with clues written on them around the valley, and we have to go and find them. When we've solved all the clues, we get the treasure."

"What are clues?" asked Rosa.

"It's something that helps you solve a problem or mystery," Pat continued.

Rosa still looked puzzled.

"When do we go on this, treasure hunt?" asked Anna.

"On Sunday afternoon, it's Thursday today, then its Friday, Saturday and the next day is Sunday," said Penny. Bicycles always have trouble remembering the days of the week!

Pat returned the letter to school the following day and Mrs Page told the class that they would be in teams of four, and to arrive 10 minutes before the start, so they would have time to find their team.

Sunday morning soon arrived and began with Mr Stamp opening the Post Office as usual so visitors could buy souvenirs. Just after lunch Pat went to see Anna.

"Is it time to go now?" asked Anna.

"No, not yet," said Pat. "Come on let's go for a ride."

Pat pulled Anna out of the shed and they pedalled down the path of the Post Office and on to the main street.

"We might see the teachers hiding the clues," said Anna.

"That's cheating," said Pat. "But we might," she thought to herself.

They rode round the village, but didn't see any of the teachers or pieces of paper. By the time they got back to the Post Office, Penny and Rosa were waiting.

"Where have you two been? It's time to go now," said Penny angrily.

"We just went for a ride that's all," said Anna. "Let's go and meet Andrew and Robert at school."

When all the children and bicycles were outside the school Mrs Page rang the school bell and said, "Will you please get in to your teams and choose a captain."

Pat, Penny, Andrew and Robert along with their bicycles Anna, Rosa, Spokes and Skid stood together in a circle.

"Whose going to be captain?" asked Andrew.

"I want to be captain," said Pat.

"You always want to be captain," said Penny.

"I am the eldest," replied Pat.

"I know but it isn't fair," muttered Penny to herself. She knew there was no point in arguing. The boys agreed that Pat should be captain, but that they should all help to solve the clues.

"Are you all ready now?" shouted Mrs Page. "For those children who have never been on a treasure hunt before, this is what you have to do. There are three teams and each team has four clues to solve, but you will all be looking for the same treasure."

The team captains were each given a different coloured sealed envelope.

"Now, boys and girls when I ring the bell, you may open the envelope. Inside is your first clue, which will lead you to the second and so on until you reach the treasure. Take care and good luck," continued Mrs Page.

The bell rang and Pat quickly ripped open the blue envelope.

"Hurry up," said Robert.

"Alright, I'm going as fast as I can. Here it is, now listen," Pat held up a blue piece of paper and read.

Your first, is near the tallest
And one of the wettest
Keep going up the lane
A simple clue, to test the brain
By the road, what can you see
The clue is next to the…..

"What?" shouted Penny," I don't understand a word of that. It’s far too difficult, I'm not playing."

"Don't be silly, let's work it out together," said Pat in her big sister voice. "The first line is 'Your first, is near the tallest', any ideas?"

"That's easy. The waterfall. Come on," said Andrew pushing Spokes down the road and jumping on the saddle as they whizzed towards the Church.

"Agh," cried Spokes. "I do wish he wouldn't do that."

Penny sat on Rosa's saddle and pedalled off after the others. "I still don't understand but never mind," Penny said to Rosa.

"Well, neither do I, but it looks like fun," replied Rosa.

As they cycled down the lane towards the waterfall, Pat repeated the rest of the clue.

Keep going up the lane
A simple clue to test the brain
By the road, what can you see
The clue is next to the.....

"Tree," shouted Penny as she pedalled quickly to catch up.

"Yes, tree, there is a tree by the road next to the path, that goes to waterfall" shouted Rosa.

Andrew and Robert looked at each other. "I think she's getting the idea," they said together.

They all smiled, and with great speed raced to the waterfall. Robert arrived first on his bicycle, he called Skid. As they got nearer to the tree, Skid closed his eyes as he knew what was coming, Robert jumped off, before he stopped and the poor bicycle continued on, toward the wall that went round the tree.

"Ow," screamed Skid as he crashed to the ground. "It's a tough life being a boys bicycle."

Robert found the next clue just as Penny arrived.

"I've got it," he yelled.

"Quick, Robert, read it out," said Andrew.

A place where you stay overnight
Turn left, not right
Down to the gently flowing stream
Stay together, in your team
This clue is small, and very thin
So look carefully, to help you win.

"Hmm," said the four bicycles thoughtfully.

"Stay overnight? This is a tough one," said Pat.

They all kept mumbling, "Overnight."

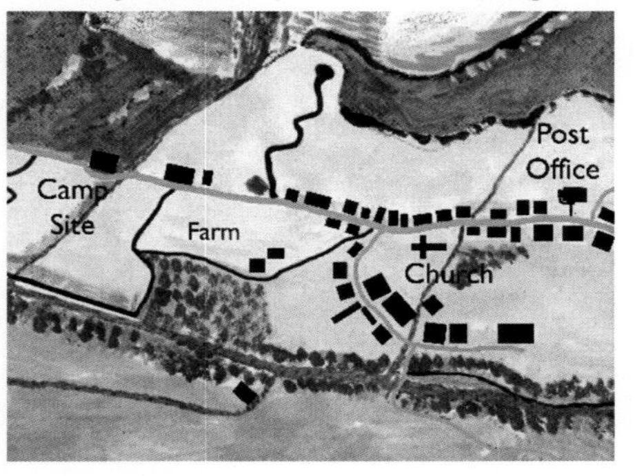

"Is there another clue? Look on the back of the paper," said Penny.

"There's just a map of Cristo, the houses, church, campsite..." said Robert.

"That's it! Campsite, visitors stay overnight," shrieked Pat jumping up and down with delight.

"There is a bridge over the stream near the campsite," said Andrew.

As soon as the words had left Andrew's mouth the blue team were pedalling towards the campsite, and the bridge over the stream. It took about five minutes to reach the short path that led to the bridge, they left their bicycles on the grass and walked onto the bridge. There were railings on both sides of the bridge.

"It must be on the bridge somewhere," said Pat. "Penny and I will look on this side, you two try the other side and try not to fall in the stream."

The four children peered, poked, squinted and searched in every crack and hole along the bridge.

"There's nothing on this side," said Robert and Andrew.

"I'll read the clue again," said Robert. "This clue is small and very thin, so look carefully to help you win."

"I didn't find the clue but there's a piece of string hanging over there," said Penny.

"Where is it?" said Andrew.

"I'll show you," replied Penny hurrying back along the bridge.

They all arrived at a point near the end of the bridge and stared at a thin piece of blue string.

"That's not the clue," said Pat.

"Wait a minute, try pulling the string," said Robert.

All the children watched anxiously, their hearts beating faster and faster, as more string was pulled up. Soon a piece of blue paper appeared.

"That’s it! Well done!" shouted Andrew.

"Well done to everyone," smiled Pat. "Read the clue, Penny."

> The third clue you will like
> Time to get, back on your bike
> It can be seen, but not spoke
> A place for cycling folk
> Look among the chains and tyres
> For the clue, fastened to the hires.

The four children walked back to their bicycles thinking about the third clue.

"Well, did you find it?" said Anna sternly. "It's alright for you, but it's boring for us, waiting here, while you have all the fun."

"Sorry," said Pat, "You bicycles can solve the next clue."

Penny read out the third clue once again, and all the bicycles stood in a circle whispering to each other.

"Are you ready yet?" asked Pat.

"Yes," said Rosa, "Spokes has the answer."

"Follow me," shouted Spokes.

With a sudden rush all the bicycles and riders were racing back towards the village.

"Where are we going?" asked Pat.

"You'll have to wait and see," replied Anna.

As they were cycling down the main street Spokes suddenly shouted, "Stop! We're here."

The four bicycles stopped outside Mr Wheeler's Cycle Hire shop.

"Here?" asked Robert. "How did you solve the clue to bring us here?"

"Well, it's all about cycling, with spokes on the wheels, chains and tyres and the hire shop is Mr Wheeler's," explained Rosa.

Pat and Penny looked at each other most impressed.

"All we need now, is the next clue," said Rosa. "If you wheel us to the hire bicycles, we'll ask which one of them has the clue."

Anna and Rosa went to the first row, and Spokes and Skid, to the second row. There was a lot of chattering and chains rattling with laughter as all the bicycles were told about the treasure hunt. The problem was that none of the bicycles had the clue. Anna and Rosa were just about to give up searching when Rosa heard a little voice shouting, "I've got the clue." Penny and Rosa looked at the front of the shop and there, tied to the smallest bicycle in Cristo, was the last clue.

"Thank you little bicycle," said Penny.

Penny took the last clue to Andrew.

"Would you like to read the last clue?" she asked.

Andrew opened the blue envelope and read.

> The treasure is where you post a letter
> Not just a cup but something better
> You need to search high and low
> Just a little reminder, of a visit to Cristo

"To the Post Office," shouted Pat and Penny together, much to the amusement of the people outside the shop.

Mr Wheeler's shop is quite near the Post Office, so it wasn't long before they were standing by the post box.

"This is where you post a letter," remarked Robert. "What's the next line again?"

"Not just a cup but something better," read Andrew once again.

"I think you need to go inside," said Anna.

"Perhaps you're right. Come on, let's go and look in the Post Office shop," said Pat.

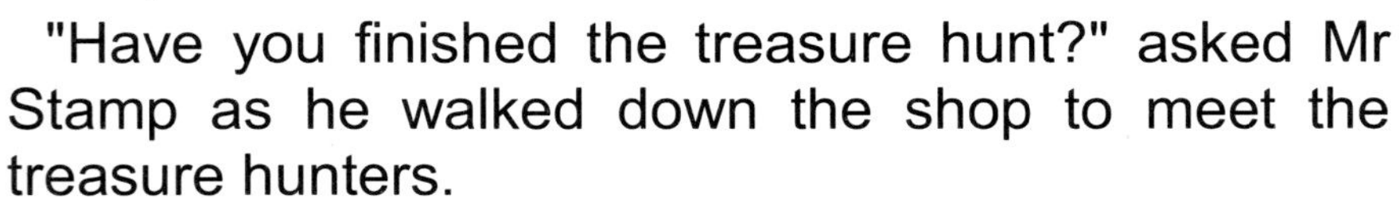

The four bicycles were parked outside while Pat, Penny, Andrew and Robert went inside.

"Hi Dad," shouted Penny.

"Have you finished the treasure hunt?" asked Mr Stamp as he walked down the shop to meet the treasure hunters.

"No, the last clue says we have to come here," said Robert.

"Oh, really?" said Mr Stamp pretending not know anything about it.

"Dad, do you know what the treasure is?" asked Pat.

"I might," said Mr Stamp. "But you have to solve the clues for yourselves."

Andrew read out the whole clue once more, slowly they mumbled the words over and over to themselves.

"Not a cup. What is like a cup? asked Andrew.

"A glass," said Penny.

"A mug," said Robert.

"A mug! Yes a mug! A mug from Cristo, that's what we're looking for!" said Andrew jumping up and down.

"Yes, of course! And I know where they are," said Pat joining in the jumping about.

Pat led the way to a large display of souvenir mugs.

"Here they are. I remember because I nearly knocked them over," continued Pat.

"We've found the treasure. It's a mug!" shouted Penny as they ran outside to tell Rosa and the other bicycles.

Mr Stamp heard all the excitement and came out to check their clues.

"Well done all of you," he said. "You can each take a mug home, but remember the other teams haven't finished yet, so don't let them see the mugs."

"Thanks Dad," said Pat and Penny.

"Thanks Mr Stamp," said Andrew and Robert.

"Let's go back to school and see who else has finished," said Pat.

Just as they were leaving the green team arrived at the post box.

"Quick hide the mugs," whispered Robert.

All four mugs quickly disappeared, up jumpers, down trousers and Robert pushed his under his baseball cap.

The green team didn't take much notice of the giggling bicycles, or the four children with lumps and bumps, as they ran in to the Post Office.

After returning to the school playground and finding out they were the second team to finish, Andrew and Robert went home to tell their parents all about the treasure hunt whilst Pat, Penny, Anna and Rosa slowly cycled back to the shed at the side of the Post Office.

"I enjoyed that," said Penny.

"Yes, that really was brill," said Pat. "Let's go and tell Mum all about the treasure hunt."

The Cycle Race

It was the last Saturday of the school summer holidays. Pat and Penny were fast asleep in bed and Mr Stamp had gone downstairs to have his breakfast, before going out to deliver the letters and parcels. He made himself a cup of tea and some toast, switched on the radio, and sat down at the table. The voice on the radio said:

"... and that was the news. Next, today's weather. It will be cloudy to start with, but, brighter, sunny weather will move in from the south giving all places a sunny afternoon ..."

"That's a change after last week's rain," thought Mr Stamp.

"...you're listening to Peaks Radio," continued the voice. "Today's lunchtime show will be coming live, from the Annual Cycle Race in Cristo..."

"The what!" shouted Mr Stamp. "Oh, no! I'd forgotten all about the race. I'd better hurry. Mr Wheeler asked me to deliver the entry forms yesterday, and they are still here."

He ran out of the house with a piece of toast in one hand, and his post bag in the other.

Mrs Stamp was the next to wake up. After getting dressed she went into see Pat and Penny who were still asleep.

"Come on you two, wake up! Time for breakfast. It's the Cycle Race today, Anna and Rosa are waiting for you. They need to be cleaned, oiled and don't forget to check the air in their tyres," she said.

"Alright Mum. We're coming," Pat and Penny said together.

After breakfast Pat went to find the oilcan, whilst Penny asked her Mum for some hot soapy water and a sponge to wash their bicycles. They met outside the shed, where they could hear Anna and Rosa chattering about the race.

"Good morning," said Pat.

"You two are talking a lot this morning," said Penny.

"Well, Rosa says she wants Cona, from Cycle Hire Shop in our team, and I keep telling her she can't, because Tracks is coming," said Anna.

"That's right," said Pat. "Our cousin Michael and his bicycle, Tracks are coming today, and they want to be in our team.

Both bicycles were wheeled outside the shed to be washed. There was a lot of laughing and giggling as Anna and Rosa were washed. "Please don't wash under my handle bars, you know it tickles me," laughed Rosa.

The laughing suddenly stopped when a voice shouted, "Hello."

"Who's that?" asked Penny.

"It's cousin Michael," Pat said. "Where's Tracks?"

He's outside the front of the Post Office with my Mum and Dad," said Michael. "I'll go and get him."

They finished washing Anna and Rosa and waited until Michael came back with Tracks. Tracks was a black 'BMX' bike, with big chunky tyres and padding on the handle bars.

"Wow," said Penny. "Look at him, I've never seen a bicycle like that before. Doesn't he look smart?"

Tracks swayed gently from side to side as Michael pushed him across the path, he was trying to make himself look as tough as possible.

"Huh, what does he look like?" sniffed Anna, unimpressed.

Pat and Penny continued getting Anna and Rosa ready for the race, whilst they chatted to Michael about what had happened since they last met. Then Pat asked, "How was the journey?"

"Some people from the radio interviewed us," said Tracks.

"That's right, I was on the radio this morning. Did you hear me?" asked Michael. "Well the man from Peaks Radio asked me if I was going to be in the

Cycle Race. I told him I was going to be in a team with my cousins, Pat and Penny."

"You mentioned us!" said Pat. "I wonder if Mum heard it."

Just then Mr Stamp came back from delivering the entry forms for the race. There were just three left, one for Pat, one for Penny and one for Michael.

"Here are your entry forms for the race. You have to put your name, and the name of your bicycle on the form," said Mr Stamp. "When you have done that, take it to Mr Wheeler's shop and enter the race for small bicycles."

The children quickly wrote their names on the entry forms, and were soon pedalling to Mr Wheeler's shop. There were more people outside the shop than Anna and Rosa had ever seen.

"You wait here," said Pat. "I'll take the entry forms in, and get our numbers."

"I've never been in the race before," said Tracks," What happens?"

"There are actually two races, one for the big bikes, who start first so we little bicycles don't get knocked over, and another race for us," explained Pat.

"That's not fair. If they go first, they'll win," said Tracks.

"Ah, but they have to go round twice, we only have to go round once," said Penny.

It wasn't long before Pat came back with three pieces of paper and some string.

"We have to tie these numbers to our bicycles," she said." There's twenty, twenty-one and twenty-two."

"Can I have number twenty?" asked Rosa.

"Number twenty-one please!" said Tracks.

"That leaves us with twenty-two," Pat told Anna.

Michael tied the numbers on to the handle bars and then they slowly made their way to the starting area where all the Mums and Dads were waiting.

When everyone had their numbers tied on to their bicycles, and looked as if they were ready, Mr Wheeler went and stood on a small black box, which had been placed at the side of the road, next to the starting line.

"Will all the large bikes, please come to the starting line," he shouted at the top of his voice. "The rules of the race are quite simple, you will start first and go round the course twice, little bicycles will go round once, does everyone understand?" he continued.

There was a short silence as the riders nodded their heads.

After checking that all the bikes were behind the line, Mr Wheeler picked up a large green flag and shouted.

"Is everybody ready?"

He then lifted the flag high into the air and shouted

"Ready, steady, go..," he then quickly lowered the flag. The first group raced away leaving the crowd cheering.

The big bikes went straight up the road and it wasn't long before they were turning the first corner.

Mr Wheeler shouted, "Will all the small bicycles come to the starting line."

Anna, Rosa and Tracks had all agreed to stay together and not race too quickly, otherwise they would soon get tired and have to leave the race.

Pat, Penny and Michael pushed their bicycles to the start line. They sat on the saddles, one foot ready on the pedal, both hands tightly gripping the handle bars ready for action.

Pat and Penny's chains were rattling with excitement while Tracks moved backwards and forwards nervously.

Once again, Mr Wheeler checked that all the bicycles were behind the line before raising his flag,

"Ready, steady, go!" he shouted, lowering the flag as he said go.

Anna was the fastest to start followed by Tracks, Rosa and the other bicycles a little way behind. Most of the bicycles were in a group as they pedalled round the first corner and headed towards the church.

"Main Street. This is the right way," said Pat as she followed the plan her Mum had given her. "We go along here and then straight on, past the farm, past the end of the village, and then right towards the woods."

Pat and Penny pedalled as fast as their legs could go, while Anna and Rosa kept blinking their eyes trying to keep the wind out.

"Faster, faster," everyone chanted.

"We can't let the big bikes catch up," shouted Michael.

"Faster, faster," everyone chanted.

"Don't worry, they have to go round twice, and we're nearly half way round now," said Penny.

At that moment the leading group of six bikes could be heard not far behind. Both groups came to the corner together. There was shouting and screaming, bells ringing and hooters hooting. It was chaos. Tracks went out of control disappearing into the ditch. Anna and Rosa bumped into each other but managed not to fall over. The big bikes pushed their way through and raced off.

"Bully!" shouted Tracks. "I hope your wheels drop off," shouted Rosa. "Road hog!" shouted Anna.

The small bicycles and riders got up, dusted themselves down and checked for bumps, bruises, bent wheels and crooked handle bars. Sam came staggering out of the hedge and joined the group as they continued along the road towards the double bend.

"Shh, everybody," Michael said. "Can you hear anything?"

"No" replied Pat. "Why?"

"It's quiet," said Michael. "Before we could hear the young men shouting, and now it's quiet."

"Yes, that is funny," thought Anna.

Pat arrived at the first bend in the woods and heard groaning noises, she cautiously pedalled round the second corner and saw what had happened. The six leading bikes had crashed into the back of the slowest group of bikers who had been taking it easy round the course.

Anna and Pat skidded to a halt and went to see if they could help. There was a right mess. Bicycles were tangled up with each other and bikes were sticking out of hedges, bushes and fences. There was even a rider hanging from a tree.

The other children and small bicycles soon arrived, and quickly went to help the wounded riders. Two of the boys lifted Rosa over the broken bikes so that Penny could ride into the village and get help.

Pat was the eldest of the children and began organising the rescue.

"Michael, you see if you can get that man out of the tree. I will try and stop that man's head bleeding," she said.

By this time Penny was just outside the village and people were cheering her and Rosa all the way.

"Help! Help!" Penny shouted.

But everyone was cheering so loud they couldn't hear her shouting, people began to look puzzled when they realised Rosa was the only bicycle in sight.

"Help! Help!" she continued.

Rosa came speeding round the last corner, and across the finishing line, straight into Mr Stamp, nearly knocking him over.

"What's the matter? Where is everyone?" he asked.

Penny was quite out of breath.

"There's been, huh, huh," she puffed.

"There's been a terrible, huh, huh."

"A terrible accident,"

"Calm down, now take you time. Accident, what accident?' asked Mr Stamp calmly.

"A terrible accident, you must go and help, in the woods, please," Penny said still out of breath.

News of what had happened soon spread through the crowd and it wasn't long before people were running back up the lane. The doctor went back to his house to collect his medical bag and lots of bandages.

It was nearly an hour before everything was cleared up and the wounded riders were on their way home. Most of the riders just had bumps and bruises, there was just one rider who had a cut head which needed stitches.

"Well that's that," said Pat to Michael. "I suppose we had better go back now."

All the small bicycles pedalled slowly to the village together, as they turned the corner into the main street near Mr Wheeler's shop the people cheered. The children and their bicycles were smiling proudly as everyone gathered around our small group of heroes at the finishing line.

Mr Wheeler stood on his black box once more and raised his arms asking the crowd to be quiet.

"According to the rules of the race, the first rider to cross the finish line is the winner," he shouted. "That was Penny Stamp, of course!"

There was loud cheer from the crowd, Penny and Rosa smiled and blushed.

"But as you all know there was a terrible accident in the woods, and while Penny was the first to cross the finish line, it wouldn't be fair to award the trophy to her," he continued.

"So I have decided that instead of their being one winner, there will be lots of winners. All the small bicycles are the winners, and I would like Patricia Stamp as the eldest of the winners to come and collect the trophy, which will be kept at school until next year."

Pat pushed Anna through the crowd to where Mr Wheeler was standing. Everyone clapped and cheered as the shiny trophy was presented to Pat, she turned round and lifted it as high as she could. She'd seen them do it on television. All the small bicycles then stood together and had their photograph taken.

This really had been a day to remember.

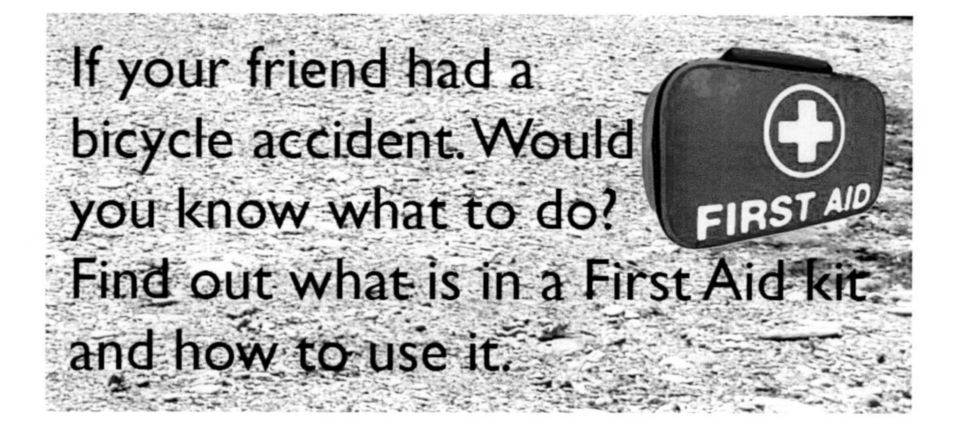

The Mountain Drive

The summer season was coming to an end with only a few visitors in Cristo. The school holidays had finished and all the children were back at school. It was the time of year when everyone had begun getting ready for winter. Most people were not looking forward to long dark nights but until the clocks went back everybody liked to think it was summer.

The first week in September was a very special time for Mr Bull, the farmer, and the people in the village of Cristo. Each year in spring after the snow has melted, all the cows are moved up the valley to the mountain meadow.

Mr Bull can cut the grass in Cristo for the cows to eat in winter. This has been the tradition for hundreds of years and the days the cows leave the village in spring and when they return in autumn are special days.

It was Saturday morning and Pat had just woken, Penny was already eating her breakfast when Pat came into the kitchen.

"You know what today is don't you?" said Pat.

"Saturday," replied Penny. "I'm sure I should know this but give me a clue?

"One word. Cows," said Pat.

"Cows?" said Penny. "Why cows, and Saturday? We don't have any cows and Mr Bull's cows are all in the mountain meadow. Ah, I know, it's time for the cows to come home."

"Yes and it's our turn to go and bring them down from the mountain," said Pat.

"Why didn't I know this?" asked Penny.

"Because only a few children can go each year and I didn't want you telling everyone," said Pat.

"I wouldn't do that," said Penny.

Pat gave Penny one of those knowing looks that an older sister gives when they know they are right. At that moment Mrs Stamp came in.

"Come on girls. You have one hour before the long walk with Mr Bull up the mountain," said Mrs Stamp. "Pat has a list of what you need, so eat your breakfast and pack your bag for tonight."

As they packed, Pat explained that they would be travelling for two hours, staying in the mountain farm house tonight and then leading the goats in the mountain drive.

"Penny, one more thing. You will need your traditional costume," said Pat.

Penny stood completely still with a look of shock on her face.

"Nobody said anything about wearing a dress and not that dress," said Penny.

Pat was busy packing her bag and smiling as she knew what Penny would say about the dress, and that was the real reason why she didn't tell her.

"You can wear jeans and jumper today and the dress tomorrow," said Pat. "Come on, everyone else will be dressed up. This is a special day, don't spoil things."

"I know, people have been doing this for hundreds of years and I'm only following tradition," said Penny. "But I don't want to wear that dress."

With that the dress went flying across the room. The ruck sack was zipped up and Penny stormed out of the room.

"I'm going to collect Rosa or haven't you told them either," said Penny angrily.

"Well actually. No," said Pat.

As the older sister it was left to Pat to pack the dress in her bag, as Penny would be wearing it tomorrow. By the time Pat arrived at the shed Penny had told Anna and Rosa about going up the mountain.

A while later, Pat, Penny, Anna and Rosa met Mr Bull and Billy, Mr Bull's son, and some more men from the village who would be helping with the cows. Soon everyone was ready and with Mr Bull leading the way, off they went.

The journey along the valley is mainly flat with just a few small hills. This made cycling very easy and was a journey that Pat and Penny had made many times. With Billy, Mr Bull and his men walking, cycling was even easier.

After about half an hour Pat and Penny were the first to arrive at the bottom of the ski lift.

"Here we are," said Anna. "Now we can have a ride."

Pat and Penny looked at each other, smiled and kept on cycling.

"Wow, wow, wow," said Rosa trying to put the brakes on. "We've gone past the lift."

"Yes, that's because we are not going that way to Mr White's hut," said Pat. "We are going to the lake to bring back the cows."

"And the goats," said Penny.

"Just how far is the lake?" asked Rosa.

"You'll see when we get there," replied Penny.

At that point everyone arrived at the gate and cattle grid at the bottom of the hill which led to the lake. A little further along the sign said Cristo Lake 1 Hour 30 Mins.

Anna and Rosa looked at the road and the hill horror.

"We can't go up there," said Rosa.

"Of course you can, change your gear to number one and we'll all pedal together," said Pat.

With Pat pedalling Anna and Penny pedalling Rosa they set off up the hill.

Mr Bull and all the other people walked behind but as the journey went on slowly the men caught up and went past the two cyclists.

"Can we, can we have a rest?" shouted a breathless Pat.

Mr Bull looked round and said, "There is a seat round the next bend, we can stop there."

After a short rest, more cycling and pushing, more rests and pushing, they finally arrived at the lake.

"Oh it's beautiful," said Anna. "I've never been here before."

Mr Bull stopped and said, "We have a busy two days. For those of you that haven't been here before, the house is at the far side of the lake and the barns are here. Pat, Penny and Billy, you go and find the goats and bring them to the barn."

"What are goats?" asked Rosa.

"I will show you when we see one," said Billy. "We are looking for eight goats."

The men went to the barn and began cleaning up and loading the cheese making equipment onto the wagon.

Shall we leave Anna and Rosa here while we look for the goats?" asked Billy.

"No, we would like to help," said Anna.

"Okay. This way then," said Billy.

The three children and two bicycles set off along the path that ran round the edge of the lake, looking for goats.

"I've seen one," said Rosa who up until that point didn't know what a goat looked like.

"Where," said Billy.

"There, in front with horns," said Rosa.

"That's a cow," said Pat. "The men will collect the cows later. We are looking for a small white animal with no horns."

"Okay, I will look," said Rosa.

About half way round the lake Billy said, "Let's stop and listen, the goats have small bells round their necks so we should be able the hear them."

They all stood still, only the sound of the wind in the trees and the gentle lap of water from the lake could be heard.

"Ssh, listen," said Penny. "Over there, I can hear something."

Billy walked slowly toward the faint sound and called, "Oye-er."

At that point a little white head popped up from behind a rock.

"Oye-er," called Billy again and the goat came walking toward him.

"That's a goat!" said Rosa.

"Yes, what did you think they looked like?" asked Pat.

"I was looking for something smaller," said Rosa. "I've seen lots of those animals you call goats back there."

Rosa turned round and with Penny pedalling they went back along the path. Rosa quickly put on her brakes, nearly throwing Penny to the ground.

"There!" said Rosa.

"Sure enough sitting near a rock there were six goats, gently munching grass and enjoying the view of the lake.

Billy who was a little out of breath from running shouted, "Oye-er."

The goats looked up, continued chewing and slowly trotted to the path to meet Billy.

"Six are here and one over there means one more to find," said Billy. "Now we all know what a goat looks like, has anyone seen the last goat anywhere?"

Everyone shook their head, no.

"I will keep these seven goats together as they know me," said Billy. "Pat and Penny will you go ahead and look for the last goat?"

"Will do," said Pat and Penny together.

They cycled ahead looking left and right, behind rocks and trees near the edge of the lake but there was no sign of the goat.

Pat shouted, "Oye-er!" Just like Billy, had been doing.

"Maybe it has run away," said Penny.

"Or been eaten by a dragon," said Anna.

"Don't be silly, there no such things as dragons," said Pat.

Anna and Rosa winked at each other and continued looking.

It was beginning to get late, and time they were back at the barn.

Billy said, "We will have to look tomorrow for the last goat. It will be dark soon."

With Billy leading the way, Pat and Anna on one side and Penny and Rosa on the other they walked with the seven goats to the barn where Mr Bull had prepared a small field to keep the goats in until tomorrow. A short while later Mr Bull appeared with goat number eight.

"Where did you find that goat?" asked Billy

"This one has been ill, so I've been looking after it," said Mr Bull.

"We've been searching all over for that," said Pat.

"Come on let's go to the house," said Billy.

The house wasn't built for many people, so after dinner some were able to sleep in beds, while the others had to sleep on the floor.

The next morning everyone was up early and after breakfast began packing and finishing cleaning the barns ready for the mountain drive.

When the cows are in the mountains during the summer they have a bell round their neck. This helps the farmer find any cows that may be lost.

On special occasions the bells are changed, the largest cows get the largest bells and will lead the procession, other cows get smaller bells.

"Billy," called Mr Bull. "Will you wash all the goats? They need to be clean and white. We are going to round up the cows."

"Okay, Dad," said Billy. "Pat, will you and Anna cycle back to the house and get some warm soapy water. Penny, bring Rosa and we can take the bells off and polish them."

It was hard work polishing, but great fun washing the goats, even if it was a bit smelly! When they were all washed and dried, and the bells back around their necks they looked splendid.

Pat, still with her sleeves rolled up, turned to the goats and said, "You all look beautiful, so stay that way." Pointing her finger at each one in turn. "And no mess, I'm not washing anymore bottoms today."

Mr Bull came over to check everything was finished and said, "Well done, all nice and clean. You three go and get something to eat and get changed, I will put the two bicycles on the wagon ready for the journey."

"Oh, good, we can have a ride back," said Rosa.

After some bread and cheese sandwiches and a drink, Penny got up and went to see Anna and Rosa.

"Are you alright up there?" asked Penny.

"We are a bit squashed between all these wooden things and they do smell of cheese, but we are fine," said Anna.

"Are you going to get dressed up like everyone else?" asked Rosa.

"No, I said I wouldn't wear the dress and it's still in Cristo," said Penny feeling sad. "I will be the odd one out and feel silly walking at the front in jeans and a jumper."

At that moment Pat arrived in her dress and carrying her bag and Penny's ruck sack, only to find Penny crying to herself and leaning on the wagon.

"Penny's very sad," said Rosa. "She has left her dress in Cristo."

Pat went to Penny, put her arm round her and said. "What's the matter?"

"I, I am very silly," she sobbed. "You, are all dressed up and I, I, look like a farm girl."

"Come here," said Pat in a comforting voice. "I knew this would happen so I packed your dress in my bag, here off you go and get changed."

Penny wiped the tears from her eyes, looked at Pat and smiled.

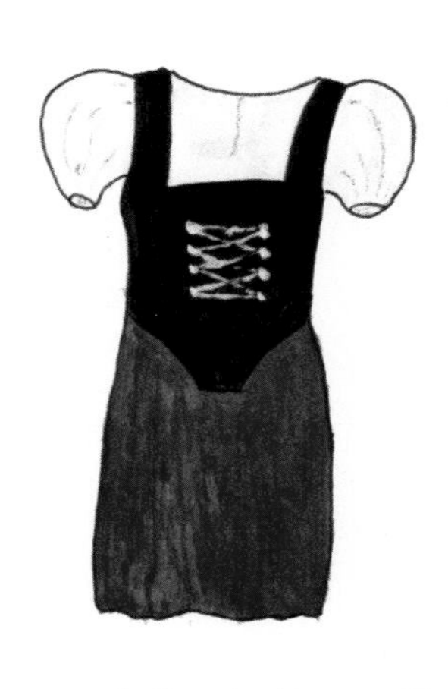

"You've saved me," said Penny. "You're my best sister."

She took the dress and ran to the house.

"Best sister," thought Pat as she smiled. "Hang on, I'm the only sister, she is cheeky."

Soon everyone was ready. Billy went first, then the goats with Pat and Penny looking beautiful in their matching red and black dresses. Next came Mr Bull with the three largest cows each one wearing a huge bell which went dong, dong as they walked. Next came the other cows and the men. At the back was the wagon carrying all the cheese making equipment with Anna and Rosa somewhere in the middle.

It took a long time to walk down the hill to where the valley was flat and as they got nearer and nearer to Cristo, Billy could see David from school with his bicycle.

"They're coming," said David to himself, jumping on the saddle and pedalling as fast as he could go. As he got to the village he shouted. "They're coming. Get ready everyone, they're nearly here, they're coming."

"The church bell began to ring and everyone came out onto the road leading to the farm.

"Listen," said Penny. "They're ringing the bells for us."

"Yes, and remember to wave to everyone as we walk past," said Pat.

There were a lot of people cheering and waving as the mountain drive was famous and visitors came from all over to see and hear the cows coming home. Billy had done this many times before and waved his arms like a professional. Pat and Penny took a bit of time to get used to waving and making sure the goats didn't run off.

"Hello Pat! Hello Penny!" came a voice from the crowd.

They both looked around.

"Hi Mum!" said Pat and Penny together and waving both hands and smiling.

The procession went through the village to the big gate into Mr Bull's farm.

When all the animals were safely in the field and getting down to what they do best, eating grass the men went home.

Pat and Penny went to collect Anna and Rosa and their bags, from the wagon and slowly pushed the bicycles home. Traditional dresses were not good for riding bicycles.

By the time they got home, and put Anna and Rosa back in the shed, Mr Stamp had seen the pictures that Mrs Stamp had taken.

"Hello girls, did you have a nice time?" said Mrs Stamp.

"It was very busy and hard work," said Pat.

"And messy. We had to wash the goats," said Penny.

"Come and look at these," shouted Mr Stamp.

As they walked into the front room Penny said, "Oh, Mum, you didn't take pictures of us?"

"Of course I did," said Mrs Stamp.

"Look at us," said Pat. "I think we look good."

"You do," said Mr Stamp. "You look beautiful and we are proud of you."

"Would you do it again?" said Mrs Stamp.

Pat and Penny looked at each other, smiled and said, "Yes, of course, we would."

"But I will need a larger dress size next time," said Penny.

Character List

Pat and Penny, daughters of Mr and Mrs Stamp and live at the Post Office.

Mr and Mrs Stamp, Postmaster and his wife.

Anna and Rosa, Pat and Penny's bicycles.

Mrs Page, school teacher in Cristo

Mr Wheeler, owner of the Cristo Cycle Hire Shop.

Mrs Guest, owner of the Peak View Hotel.

Mr Bull and **Billy Bull**, Cristo farmer and his son.

Michael rides **Tracks** Pat and Penny's cousin.

School children and their bicycles

Robert rides **Skid**

Andrew rides **Spokes**

The Author, himself

Hire bicycles, Bill and **Cona**